A ROOKIE BIOGRAPHY

JACQUES COUSTEAU

Man of the Oceans

By Carol Greene

CHILDRENS PRESS®
CHICAGO

This book is for Chris.

Jacques Cousteau (1910-   )

Library of Congress Cataloging-in-Publication Data

Greene, Carol.
    Jacques Cousteau : man of the oceans / by Carol Greene.
      p. cm. — (A Rookie biography)
    Includes index.
    Summary: A simple biography of the French oceanographer whose
underwater explorations have focused the world's attention on the beauty
of ocean life and the need to conserve that life.
    ISBN 0-516-04215-7
    1. Cousteau, Jacques Yves—Juvenile literature. 2. Oceanographers—
France—Biography—Juvenile literature. [1. Cousteau, Jacques Yves.
2. Oceanographers.] I. Title. II. Series: Greene, Carol. Rookie biography.
GC30.C68G74 1990
551.46′0092—dc20
[B]
[92]   90-2162
                                         CIP
                                       AC

Jacques Cousteau
is a real person.
He was born in 1910.
He has learned and taught
about life underwater.
He has learned and taught
about caring for the earth.
This is his story.

TABLE OF CONTENTS

Chapter 1   Three Wonderful Things 5

Chapter 2   Navy Man 11

Chapter 3   *Calypso* 19

Chapter 4   More Adventures............. 29

Chapter 5   Something Important 37

Important Dates 46

Index 47

Chapter 1

Three Wonderful Things

Jacques Cousteau was
a small boy in France
when he discovered
a wonderful thing—
water.

He liked to watch
ships float on it.
He liked to watch
stones sink in it.
Most of all, he liked
to *touch* water.

Opposite page: While the ocean roars above, it is calm and peaceful for the diver below.

Jacques wasn't strong.
The doctors said
he mustn't do much.
But he learned
to swim anyway.

When he was 10,
his family moved
to New York for a year.
Jacques and Pierre,
his big brother,
learned English.

The Cousteau family
lived for a year
in New York City,
one of the largest
cities in the world.

About that time,
Jacques discovered
another wonderful thing—
machines.

When he was 11,
he built a model crane.
It worked well.
When he was 13,
he built a car
that ran on batteries.

That same year,
he discovered
a third wonderful thing—
films.

He saved his money
and bought
a home-movie camera.
Then he began
to make his own films.

At school, Jacques
was bored and lazy.
He was a trouble-maker, too.
One day, he broke
17 windows.

That did it.
His parents sent him
to a strict boarding school.
To everyone's surprise,
Jacques loved it.

He began to study hard.
But he didn't forget
the three wonderful things
he had discovered.

He didn't know it then.
But someday
he would use them all—
water, machines, and films.

Jacques Cousteau would grow up to use machines, such as the windship *Aleyone*, and
to make films of his explorations and underwater adventures.

The naval port of Brest, France (above). A French navy ship gives a
21-gun salute as it enters the harbor at Havana, Cuba (below).

Chapter 2

Navy Man

In 1930, Jacques went
to France's naval academy.
He did well.

Three years later,
he joined the French navy
and sailed around the world.
Of course he took
his movie camera along.

Next he went to
the navy's flying school.
He was almost ready
to take his pilot's test.
Then he broke both arms
in a car crash.

Now he couldn't be a pilot.
But friends told him
swimming would make
his arms strong again.
So he stayed
in the navy and swam.

One day, Jacques
got some goggles.
All at once,
he could *see* underwater.
That changed his life.

He wanted to stay underwater
longer and longer.
So he began to work
on breathing machines.

In 1936,
Jacques began
studies of
the ocean
environment.

Jacques Cousteau and his wife, Simone, aboard the research ship *Calypso*.

In 1937, Jacques married
a girl called Simone.
She liked water too.
They had two little boys,
Jean-Michel and Philippe.

In 1939, World War II began.
Jacques fought the Germans.
He also became a spy.

Once he dressed up
as an enemy soldier.
He took pictures
of secret enemy papers.
Later, he got medals
for his war work.

Jacques testing a new regulator for the aqualung.

But he still found time
to work underwater.
In 1942, he built
a breathing machine
that really worked.
A man in Paris helped him.

Jacques in
New York for
the premiere
of his film
"The Silent World."

With his new aqualung,
Jacques could stay
underwater a long time.

After the war, divers
used Jacques' aqualung
to work underwater
getting rid of enemy mines.
But by then, Jacques
was off on new adventures.
His camera went with him.

Chapter 3

Calypso

Jacques wanted to explore
the sea in a new way.
He didn't want
to kill anything.
He wanted to learn
and to make films.

He tried to make his work
as safe as he could.
But there was danger.
Once he almost drowned
in an underwater cave.

Opposite page: A diver using an aqualung explores an underwater cave.

The deck of the *Calypso* is crowded
with winches, cables, and diving gear.

Soon Jacques knew
he must have his own ship.
In 1950, he got one.
He named it *Calypso*.
It had been a minesweeper—
then a car ferry.

All sorts of people
traveled on *Calypso*—
scientists and sailors,
Jacques' wife, Simone,
sometimes his children,
and the family dog.

Two divers explore a coral reef in the Red Sea.

Their first big trip
was to the Red Sea.
There they saw coral reefs
like underwater cities.
Jacques swam with bumpfish
and saw them crunch coral.

Then, near France,
they found a sunken ship
full of wine jars.
It had sunk
over 2,000 years ago.
They tasted the wine.

Off Africa, they watched
a school of whales.
They saw the others
protect a hurt whale
by swimming around it.

Jacques Cousteau (center) found these two ancient statues at the bottom of the Mediterranean Sea near Greece.

Many fish live near the coral reefs in the Indian Ocean.

In the Indian Ocean,
they dived on coral reefs.
They swam through a fairyland of
beautiful colors and shapes.

The fish had never
seen people before.
They weren't afraid.
One big grouper
became almost a pet.
They called him Jojo.

Orange and blue
sponges cling
to a coral reef
in the Indian Ocean.
A big grouper (inset)
swims nearby.

Back in the Red Sea,
they met fish so big that
they called them truckfish.

In the middle
of the Atlantic Ocean,
they found a starfish.
It lived 4½ *miles* underwater.

The sea star (left) and
the bat star (right) are
two kinds of starfish that
live in the deep oceans.

Of course someone
had to pay for these trips.
Different groups helped.
So did Jacques' films.
Sometimes the *Calypso*
worked for businesses.

Jacques began to write books,
like *The Silent World*
and *The Living Sea*.
Some became films, too,
and won Oscars.

At last, Jacques quit
the French navy.
He had too many
other things to do now.

Jacques kept in touch with the crew in their underwater home by radio and TV (right). The crew returns to the surface (below).

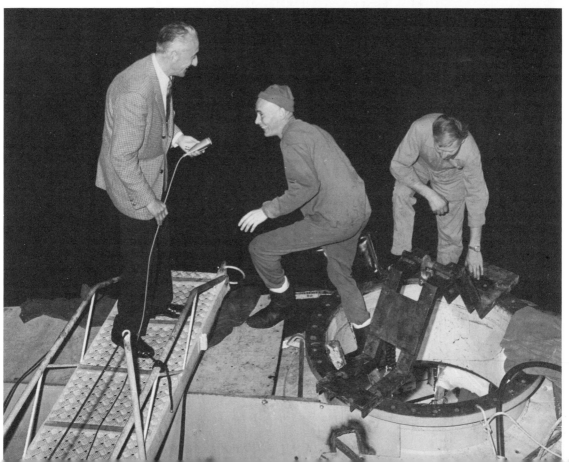

Chapter 4

More Adventures

Can people live on
the bottom of the sea?
Jacques said yes.
They could live there
and work there, too.

He called his first
underwater home Conshelf 1.
It looked like
a yellow barrel.
Two men spent a week in it.
They even had radio and TV.

The *Calypso* tows a floating research island
into place in the Mediterranean.

Conshelf 2 and Conshelf 3
were bigger and went deeper.
The men who lived
in them learned a lot.

But at last Jacques decided
that people shouldn't live
underwater all the time.

By now, his work
had made him famous.
He was asked
to make a TV series.
Jacques loved that idea.

Jacques Cousteau (left) and diver
Bernard Delemotte (right) examine a small grouper.

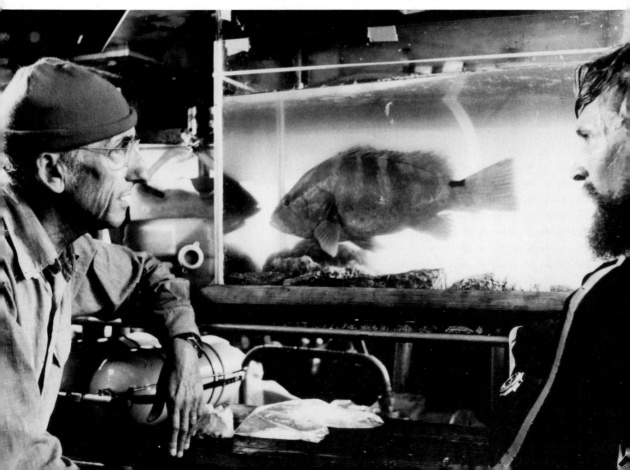

Jacques on *Calypso*, which was leaving for a
four-year research voyage around the world

He went all over the world.
He filmed sharks and whales,
dolphins and sea turtles.
He made shows about
coral reefs, sunken treasure,
octopuses, and penguins.

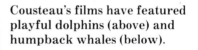

Cousteau's films have featured playful dolphins (above) and humpback whales (below).

The *Calypso* was caught in a dangerous blizzard at Hope Bay, Antarctica.

Of course he had problems.
Once, *Calypso* got caught
in a war. Another time,
the ship was chased by a typhoon.
Finding enough money
was always a problem.

Some scientists felt
Jacques' work was wrong.
They felt *real* scientists
shouldn't try to teach
people who aren't scientists.

But Jacques knew
he was right.
He had something
important to teach,
and *everyone* must
hear about it.

Cousteau (left) shows Princess Grace (center) and Prince Rainier (right) of Monaco the exhibits in the Oceanographic Museum of Monaco.

Cousteau was saddened by water
pollution that kills fish (above
left) and by trash littering
the shoreline (above right).
Cousteau saw fishermen (bottom
left and right) killing hundreds
of dolphins in their nets.

Chapter 5

Something Important

Jacques saw many things
as he traveled.
Some were beautiful.
Some were not.

He saw trash dumped
into the water everywhere.
He saw people fishing
in ways that killed
everything around.

People in Africa (left) are starving because the land is misused.
Oil spills (right) destroy life in the oceans and on the shores.

He saw oil spills.
He saw people starving
because other people
ruined their water and land.
And he saw selfish people
who just didn't care.

Jacques knew that
the earth needs its oceans.
He knew that countries
must work together
to save the oceans.

Clean oceans are vital to the health of our planet.

Jacques Cousteau's books have been published in many languages.

He told people about this
in his books and films.
He made speeches, too.
In 1974, he started
the Cousteau Society
to protect ocean life.

Philippe Cousteau (below).

Above: Jacques Cousteau (left) and
his son Jean-Michel (right).

In 1978, his son Philippe
died in a helicopter crash.
Jacques couldn't even
talk about that.
He just worked harder.
His son Jean-Michel helped.

In the 1980s, Jacques
made more trips and films.
He went to South America.
He studied life in
the Mississippi River.
He visited Haiti.

Jean-Michel Cousteau (below left) and Jacques Cousteau
(below right) visit with a giant river otter during a trip
to the Amazon River region in South America.

In 1989
Jacques was
honored by
France with
membership
in the
French Academy.

In 1985, President Reagan
gave him the Medal of Freedom.
That was a great honor.
But most of all,
Jacques Cousteau wants
people to listen to him.

Jacques Cousteau speaking at the French Academy (above left), visiting the Monaco
Oceanographic Museum (above right), where he is director, and meeting with
presidential candidate Jimmy Carter at United Nations headquarters
in New York City (below).

Cousteau in Paris, posing in front of a
giant balloon representing a blue whale

He wants them to love
and care for the earth
and its oceans.
He believes in children
and wants them to have
a healthy, beautiful planet.

Important Dates

1910   June 11—Born in Saint-André-de-Cubzac, France, to Daniel and Elizabeth Cousteau

1930   Went to École Navale (Naval Academy) at Brest

1937   Married Simone Melchoir

1942   Built the first aqualung

1950   Got his own ship, the *Calypso*

1962   Worked with Conshelf 1

1967   Began work on TV series, "The Undersea World of Jacques Cousteau"

1974   Began the Cousteau Society

1985   Received the Medal of Freedom

INDEX

Page numbers in boldface type indicate illustrations.

Africa, 23
aqualung, 4, 16-17, **16**, 18
Atlantic Ocean, 26
books, 27, 40, **40**
Brest, France, **10**
bumpfish, 22
Calypso, 14, 20, 21, 27, 30, 32, 34, **34**
Conshelf 1, 29
Conshelf 2, 30
Conshelf 3, 30
coral reefs, 22, **22**, 24, **24**, **25**, 32
Cousteau, Jean-Michel, 14, 41, **41**, 42
Cousteau, Philippe, 14, 41, **41**
Cousteau, Pierre, 6
Cousteau, Simone, 14, **14**, 21
Cousteau, Society, 40
dolphins, 32, **33**, **36**
exploring the seas, 19, 22-26
films and filming, 7, 8, 9, 11, 17, 19,
    27, 40, 42
flying school, 12
France, 5, 11, 23
French navy, **10**, 11, 27
grouper, 25, **25**
Haiti, 42
Indian Ocean, 24
Living Sea, The (book), 27
machines, 7, 9
Medal of Freedom, 43
Mississippi River, 42

naval academy, 11
New York City, 6, **6**
octopuses, 32
oil spills, 38, **38**
Paris, France, 16, 45
penguins, 32
pictures of Jacques Cousteau, 2, **13**,
    14, **16**, **17**, **23**, **31**, **32**, **33**, **34**, **35**,
    40, **41**, **42**, **43**, **44**, **45**
pollution, **36**, **37**, 38
Reagan, President, 43
Red Sea, 22, 26
school, 8, 9
sea turtles, 32
sharks, 32
Silent world, The (book), 27
South America, 42
speeches, 40, 44
spying for France, 15
starfish, 26, **26**
sunken ship, 23
sunken treasure, **23**, 32
swimming, 6, 12, 13
teaching, 35
truckfish, 26
TV series, 31
underwater living, 28, 29-30
water, 5, 9, 14
whales, 23, 32, **33**
World War II, 15

PHOTO CREDITS

ABOUT THE AUTHOR

Carol Greene has degrees in English Literature and Musicology. She has worked in international exchange programs, as an editor, and as a teacher. She now lives in St. Louis, Missouri, and writes full-time. She has published more than eighty books. Others in the Rookie Biographies series include *Benjamin Franklin, Pocahontas, Martin Luther King, Jr., Christopher Columbus, Abraham Lincoln, Beatrix Potter, Robert E. Lee, Ludwig van Beethoven, Laura Ingalls Wilder, Jackie Robinson*, and *Daniel Boone*.